THE ROAD TO YOUR BEST SELF

Discover the Miracle Power, Uncommon Nature and Greatness in You

Dr Patrick Businge

Bestselling Author of
7 Steps to Greatness

Published by Greatness University Publishers
www.greatness-university.com

ISBN-10: 1999949420
ISBN 978-1-9999494-2-6

DEDICATION

This booklet is dedicated to you. You have something special. Take the road and discover your miracle power, uncommon nature and the greatness in you.

CONTENTS

ACKNOWLEDGEMENTS

This booklet would have not been possible without the mentoring of Les Brown: world's number one motivational speaker, Ona Brown: expert in personal transformation, Brian Tracy: bestselling author and world's top success coach, and Omar Periu: world leading wealth coach.

I am indebted to colleagues in the Les Brown Maximum Achievement Team, Brian Tracy's Mastermind Group, and to Greatness University Maximum Achievement Team. It is because of their critical friendship and moral support that I have accomplished writing this and other books.

Special thanks to my family, relatives and friends. While my father Mr George Rusoke inspired my head, my mother Stella Rusoke ignited my heart. I cannot fail to thank my wife Julian Businge and my two little children for the patience and courtesy I received whilst writing this booklet and other books. I cannot end without mentioning my students and all the great people from all over the world who have inspired me and shaped my life as an author.

Dr Patrick Businge

THE ROAD TO YOUR BEST SELF

Thank you for choosing to read 'The Road to Your Best Self'. It is based on Chapter 1 of my bestselling book '7 Steps to Greatness: Take Your Life, Studies, Career and Business to the Next Level'. I would like to start by asking you some simple yet profound questions: Who are you? Do you know what is at the core of your being? What makes you 'YOU'?

The mission to find yourself

In this booklet, I am asking you to take the first step to your best self. I am sending you on a mission to find yourself. By the time you reach the end, you will have discovered your best self and developed the mindset to take your life, education, career, relationships, business, and cause to the next level. Now is the best time for you to take the road and discover your best self.

To reach the core of your being where your best self is, you will need to have an open mind as you read this booklet. This will involve changing your mindset so that you can change your life. This will require you to stretch out of your comfort zone and step into the unknown. It will involve thinking differently and taking avenues in your life that you have never explored. Remember, at one point in our lives, we are like a blind person standing at the corner of the street waiting for some to lead us across the streets of life. It is my hope that this booklet will be your SatNav to guide you through the streets of life to your best self.

Making the necessary changes and taking your life, studies, career, business and cause to the next level will depend upon you taking action during and after reading this booklet. As you might already know, knowledge is the new currency. If you don't use it, you will not get the life you deserve. In other words, the knowledge in this booklet is practically useless without using it by taking action. If you need more help, Greatness University is there to walk with you on the path to your best self.

Called to your best self

Someone is calling you now. Do you hear the call?

Finally you have listened to the calling to find yourself and answered it. Thank you for answering the call. Now I know something about you. You are on the journey to your best self. You starting to develop a deep hunger to know your best self. Like you, I have been on a similar journey. Allow me to share my story with you.

> In the summer 2017, my wife and I were hungry to take our live, careers and businesses to the next level. We made a journey from London, UK where we were living to Miami, Florida for a life changing mentorship programme with Les Brown: the world's number one motivational speaker. This journey took a lot of time to prepare, a lot of resources, and energy from us.

Dr Patrick Businge

As we travelled from London to Miami through Toronto, we met a lot of amazing people that we had never seen. We went through a lot of new places we have never been. Going through various 21st century airports, border posts with cutting age technology, and patiently waiting in the mazy queues, I was touched by the constancy of the questions asked of me and other passengers.

Who are you? Where have you been? Why are you here? Where are you going? How will you get there? What will you do when you get there?

Over time, it became clear that if we wanted to arrive at our destination, we had to honestly answer these questions. As you travel to your best self, as you go through the various border posts in your life, as you patiently queue to discover yourself so that you can live your dreams, I want to ask you these questions too. Who are you? Where have you been with your life? Why are you reading this booklet today? What brought you to this planet? Where are you going? How do you see yourself one year from now? Three years from now? Five years from now? And, what does the future look like for you? How will you get there? Who will you go with? Will it be your best self? Your dreams? Your gifts? Your talents?

On our journey, when we honestly answered these questions, we were allowed to reach our destination: Florida, The Sunshine State.

In 'The Road to Your Best Self', I will only focus on one question: Who are you? Today, I want to let you know that when you answer this question, you will have access to a new self. This new self will allow you to create a brand new start and ending to your life. I believe this is your time to step into yourself and discover the real you. Give it all and decide: 'It is not over until I find myself'.

Dr Patrick Businge

DISCOVER YOUR BEST SELF

Did you know that most people are not courageous and hungry to know themselves like you? Let me share with you something that might scare you. Imagine going for a funeral of a very important person in your life. You know the service is today starting at 2pm and you know where the funeral service is going to be. Before the service, everybody is invited to pay their last respects, including you. You approach the coffin and through the glass you look inside. To your surprise, it is you. Imagine - it is YOU!

It's a tragedy

Now ask yourself: If I died today, what would my eulogy look like? How would my close friends describe me? How would my work colleagues remember me? What virtues and qualities would my religious leaders use? What habits will my classmates include? Which core beliefs will my family members highlight to the mourners? A quote attributed to one of the founding fathers of the United States of America Benjamin Franklin says, 'Some people die at twenty five and aren't buried until they are seventy five'. Imagine this is true not just for some people but for many people who have already died and are waiting to be buried. What a tragedy!

'IT'S A TRAGEDY FOR ME. To see the DREAM IS OVER. And I never will forget the day we met …,' do you remember this song? It is called 'I'm gonna miss you' by Milli Vanilli. Yes, it is a big tragedy that many people have already left their bodies behind, dying without having taken the time to know themselves. That is why 'The graveyard is the richest place on earth, because it is here that you will find all the hopes and dreams that were never fulfilled, the books that were never written, the songs that were never sung, the inventions that were never shared, the cures that were never discovered, all because someone was too afraid to take that first step, keep with the problem, or determined to carry out their dream' (Les Brown).

I am sure you do not want to be like them. You desire to be different. You have realised that what you are doing now is only a small fraction of what you can do once you have discovered your best self. You can see yourself doing a million times better than now. You do not want to make your comfort zone your prison. You do not want to cruise along life guided by your limited self. You do not want to settle for less than who you are. You want to live a life of purpose and so are not satisfied with who you are today. You are craving for a different lifestyle. You want more from life. You are thirsty for a new you. You have said, 'It is not going to be a tragedy for me'.

Know thyself

Over the years, I have come to the realisation that if people want more from life, if they want to make a mark on this planet, if they want to live full and die empty, they must embark on a journey of self-discovery. The ancient Greek philosopher Socrates once said, 'Know thyself for the unexamined life is not worth living'. What a great advice that we need to know ourselves not just on the surface but on a deeper level. In his bestselling book 'The Monk Who Sold His Ferrari', Robin Sharma says, 'When you dedicate yourself to transforming your inner world your life quickly shifts from the ordinary into the realm of the extraordinary'. Following the examples of Socrates and Robin Sharma, you might wish to take a journey to your inner world, to the core of your being and discover your best self.

Once you reach there and discover your best self, you will have a chance to live full and die empty. You will develop a deep hunger to make your life a masterpiece because you are a piece of the master. Remember the famous Cherokee saying, 'When you were born, you cried and the world rejoiced. Live your life so that when you die, the world cries and you rejoice'. I am reminded of what I witnessed from 5th December 2013 when Nelson Mandela died at the age of 95. The world cried for Nelson Mandela because he made a lasting contribution as a freedom fighter, moral compass and symbol of the struggle against racial oppression in South Africa.

Sometimes wonder and ask myself, 'what will make the world cry for me when I am gone?' You too might be asking the same question. I might not know you one a personal level as you read this booklet but I might know why the world is likely to cry for you. I believe the world will shed tears for you and you will rejoice because of your best self. In this booklet, I will introduce you to three aspects of your best self. You are a miracle child. You are an uncommon person. You are a gifted gift.

You are a Miracle in Manifestation

Have you ever felt that you are miracle? Me, I have. Here is how I discovered is this aspect of my best self. Take time and follow me on this journey of thought since I would like you to start by imagining 'your life' before this life. Yes, I mean it. Your life before this one you are living on this planet. Allow yourself to wonder about the probability of your 'parents to be' ever meeting or falling in love. I am reminded of a story of two people who met at the airport. The lady was travelling to South Africa and the gentleman was going to the United States of America. The lady's flight was cancelled and as she waited for her next flight, the gentleman started talking to her. This was the beginning of a lifelong marital relationship that ended up in having two children. Had the flight to South Africa not been cancelled, these two children would not have existed.

Now take time to reflect on the circumstances surrounding your coming into this planet. Ponder on the billions of people that live on our planet. Be amazed on how out of more than 40 million sperms, only yours managed to successfully fertilise that one egg. Use your imagination and recreate the scene of you being born in the place you were born. The time you were born. The medical personnel that made it possible for a safe delivery. Use your mathematical skills to imagine what some experts say that the probability of you being born is like having 2.5 million people getting together over a game of dice and playing with a special dice with a trillion faces instead of six. Make a calculation and accept that your existence is one in over a trillion chances. Are you not a real miracle? I believe you are a miracle child.

A miracle child

Now, I would like you to go deeper and feel who you are. The fact that you are still alive and breathing. The fact that you are still here since there are many people you know who are now gone. You too could have been gone a long time ago but you have not, you are still here. As you read this booklet, think about the fact that it is not up to you to tell your heart to beat so that you continue to be alive. It is not up to you to tell the white blood cells to do what they are needed to do. It is not up to you to command the red blood cells to go where they are meant to go. It is not up to you to instruct your lungs to breathe. It is not up to you to tell your eyes to see the many colours in this world. It is not up to you to instruct your nostrils to smell, your tongue to taste and your brain to think. It is not up to you to fall asleep and wake up alive. All these activities are simultaneously happening regardless of your participation. They are happening regardless of your command since you are not their initiator. At this point, I believe that you are becoming more aware that you are a miracle child.

Miracle power

As a miracle child, you do not have to calculate how much water you need to drink to neutralise the excess salt in your body. From today henceforth, I invite you to become aware that you possess an invisible miracle power that does the calculations automatically without you having to stop. From the day you were conceived, this miracle power continues to solve every problem for you. It repairs your body. It has unlimited power to do everything that you could ever imagine. It is the sole reason you continue to be in this world. This miracle power occupies the whole of your body. It sees without eyes what our eyes have not seen. It hears what our ears have not heard. It communicates without words. This invisible miracle power in you reads your thoughts, experiences your fears, and knows your hopes and dreams. It is unhindered by distance, time or body. It never dies. It is the most powerful 'thing' in the universe. From it you live, move and have your being. Indeed you are a miracle.

On a special mission

There are moments you might not feel you are a miracle. When you run out of finances and your business is declared bankrupt. When your health deteriorates and you are told you have few days to live. When your relationship breaks down and what you thought was long-term love becomes lifetime hatred. When you fail your exams and start feeling you are not worthy of success. Even in these moments, I have a firm belief that you are a miracle on a special mission.

Now that you are becoming more aware of your miracle power, it is helpful to trust that all the things you desire and all the things you want to create in your life experience are all possible. Your past is approved. Your present is here. Your future is coming. You are committed to fully living your special mission. You are committed to making this world a better place than how you found it. Every day you wake up you are ready to leave the average lifestyle behind and becoming a better version of yourself. So, just accept that you are miracle on a special mission.

The French philosopher Theilhard de Chardin knew it and said, 'You are a spiritual being immersed in a human experience'. Robert Collier is honest in his book The Secret of the Ages by saying, 'You have within you a force against which the whole world is powerless'. One of the foremost spiritual authors Anthony de Mello is sure when he says, 'I have a treasure: the thing that I value most in life. I relive the events that led me to discover it. I think of the history of my life from the time I found this treasure…what it has done and meant to me. I stand before this treasure and I say, "Of all the things I have, you are the dearest"…I am a treasure. Someday, somewhere, someone discovered me. I should have no awareness of my worth if someone had not found it. I recall and relive the details of the finding and I am a multifaceted treasure'. This is the miracle power within you that also makes you uncommon.

You Are Uncommon

Have you ever thought of yourself as an uncommon person? Well, let me start with a short story about the twins. They were born on the same day, in the same hospital and within few minutes of each other. They grew up together, went to the same schools where they studied the same subjects. However, each time they sat their examinations, they achieved different results. When they completed their studies, they went on to create different levels of success, got married to different people and got different children.

This short story illustrates that, though the twins were similar in many ways, each of them was different and unique. I believe you too you are different irrespective of the common characteristics you share with other human beings. You are a unique and unrepeatable human being. There is no another 'you' anywhere in this immense universe. This makes you an uncommon person. You deserve to live and act in uncommon ways.

However, few people know they are uncommon. Few people live and act in uncommon ways. In fact, most people have chosen to be common. If they were to sit in the two-tier British Parliament, they would be in the

House of Commons rather than in the House of Lords. Look at it this way, the few Lords are the uncommon people selected on merit, based on their contributions to British society while those in the Commons are voted into parliament by the masses, based on their power of persuasion.

Take time to reflect on your life now. If you were allowed to sit in the British Parliament, where would you go? The House of Lords or the House of Commons? But, as you continue discover your best self, there is nothing to stop you from being uncommon. You are not going to settle for a common and average life after knowing that you have immense miracle power within you.

From today forth, I would like you to know that you are uncommon. You deserve to sit in the House of Lords. You are unique and unrepeatable. There is no one else anywhere like you. It is possible for you to live an uncommon life. Now that you know the truth of who you are, you have the power to take your life to the next level. Now that you know you are uncommon, I urge you to bypass your eyesight and tap into your mindsight and heartsight.

One of my favourite books contains a story of Moses who used his mindsight to bypass his eyesight. With his eyesight, he saw a burning bush that was on fire. With his mindsight he came to the conclusion that this bush which was on fire without burning was an uncommon bush. With his heartsight, he was not frightened by the bush but went closer to discern why this was the case.

It is during this moment that Moses discovered the miracle power behind the burning bush.

The burning bush inside you

As you search for your burning bush, you might find it helpful to reflect on these questions. How often do you use your mindsight and heartsight? Have you found the bush within you that is on fire? What about the miracle power beyond the bush burning within you? For Moses, beyond the bush was someone special calling him to live an uncommon life. This uncommon calling required Moses to perform uncommon actions and utter uncommon words.

I hope your response to the miracle power within you will be as uncommon as that given by Moses. Your response to this calling will be as uncommon as the calling. Remember, no one in this universe is going to experience life in the same way as you are experiencing it. You are who you are today because of the decisions you have made in your past. Refuse to allow your past struggles and failures become your standard. If you wish to make this transition, I would encourage you to make three decisions today and change your life. Start bypassing your eyesight and find the burning bush inside you. Next, use your mindsight to listen to the bush as it rustles while it burns. Last, follow your heartsight to go beyond the bush and live an uncommon life.

Beyond the statue

I know it is possible for you to live an uncommon life. While I was writing this book, I sought advice from my book coach Brian Tracy on how to write a great book. He advised me that in order to be a great writer, I must be a good reader. So, I embarked on searching and reading great books. In my search, I came across John Mason's book titled 'You're Born an Original Don't Die a Copy'. From this title, I was led to reflect on the extent to which I was living my life as an original. I then read other books written by the foremost spiritual guru Anthony de Mello. I was moved by his reflection on my statue that I would like to share with you:

> *A sculptor has been making a statue of you. The statue is ready and you go to his studio to have a look at it before it appears in public. He gives you the key to the room where your statue is so that you can see it for yourself and take all the time you want to examine it alone.*

> *You open the door. The room is dark. There, in the middle of the room is your statue, covered with a cloth... You walk up to the statue and take the cloth off...Then you step back and look at your statue. What is your first impression?...Are you pleased or dissatisfied?...Notice the material it is made of...Walk around it...see it from different angles...Look at it from far, then come closer and look at the details...Touch the statue... notice whether it is rough or smooth... cold or warm to the touch. What parts of the statue do*

you like?...What parts of the statue do you dislike?...

Say something to your statue...What does the statue reply?...What do you say in return?... Keep on speaking as long as you or the statue have something to say...Now become the statue...What does it feel like to be your statue?...What kind of existence do you have as the statue?'

Reading John Mason and Anthony de Mello's books have led me to question what kind of existence I am living: as a copy? Statue? Original? After reading and reflecting on this, you too might be moved to question yourself. You may be feeling like the co-founder of Apple Steve Jobs who said, 'For most of my life, I've felt that there must be more to our existence than meets the eye. This is who I am, and you can't expect me to be someone I'm not'. From this, you and I get the idea that life could be different for us if we decided to go beyond ourselves, beyond our bodies, and beyond our statues. This is only possible if we access the miracle power within us.

I believe that the universe is eagerly waiting for you to go beyond your statue. It is begging you live an uncommon life and manifest your greatness. To make this happen, here are some of the things you might consider doing. Educate yourself every day because you believe knowledge is the new currency. Read daily because you know reading is the food for the mind. See differently because you not only have eyesight but also mindsight and heartsight. With your mindsight, focus on what is going on in the stadium of your mind and not in the football stadium. With your heartsight, see what is taking place in the theatre of your heart and not in the world's famous auditoriums.

When you do this, you will live differently because you deserve it. You will refuse to be casual about life because you do not want to become a causality. You will hear differently because you are listening to a different voice within you. You will dance differently because you are listening to the beat of a different drum. You will become a light of greatness and leave your mark on the world. You will refuse to be denied because you have not given up on life. You will become unstoppable as you discover yourself.

You Are Gifted with Greatness

This is the last of your best self that I know about you. You are a gift that contains infinite gifts. It is customary in most parts of the world to get gifts on special occasions such as birthdays, graduations, and marriages. What gifts have you received on these days? Which one was your greatest gift?

I would like to reveal to you your greatest gift. I believe you are the greatest gift. The famous theologian Hans Urs von Balthasar says it best: 'What you are is God's gift to you, what you become is your gift to God'. What a cherished gift you are. This might be unsettling if you do not believe in God. Let me see if I can rephrase it: Your life is a gift and how you live it is a gift. At this point, there is no need to know where this gift comes from or to whom this gift goes to. What is important is to believe that you are a gift and embark on discovering how you are a gift.

Discover your gifts

To discover yourself as a gift, start by reflecting on these questions: What have I been doing with my life? Do I love it? What is my heart telling me? Where do my interests lie? What do I like most? What do I excel in? What do I desire to do with my life? Take time and discover yourself as a gift.

You are not only a gift but a gift that contains many other gifts. With the myriad of gifts you have, you will achieve far beyond your horizons in avenues of life you have never explored. This is what brilliant and accomplished individuals, such as the great composer Wolfgang Amadeus Mozart, the great inventor Thomas Edison, and the professional basketball player Michael Jordon, just to name a few, used their gifts to take their lives to new horizons.

Holy men and women like St Theresa of Avila, St Julian of Norwich, and St Teresa of Calcutta, followed the Holy Spirit to live their spiritual greatness in many places. You too are invited to be on this journey. With your innumerable gifts, you will go to many places that you could ever imagine. So, work towards becoming a gift that the world will be proud to have. This is your way of thanking the universe for the lovely home you have been living in. This is your way of thanking the universe for taking care of you. Do not deprive the universe from seeing your gifts.

Gifted with greatness

Robert Collier in his book Secret of the Ages goes on to write, 'Always there is something within you urging you on to bigger things, giving you no peace, no rest, no chance to be lazy…This "something" within you keeps telling you that you can do anything you want to do, be anything you want to be, have anything you want to have...'. Kurt Hahn, educator and founder of Outward Bound, once said, 'There is more in us that we know. If we can be made to see it, perhaps, for the rest of our lives, we will be unwilling to settle for less'. Then, the motivational speaker Les Brown says, 'You have something special, you have greatness within you'. 'Something within you' is your greatest gift. 'The more in you' is your greatest gift. The 'Greatness within you' is your greatest gift.

I believe your greatness is patiently waiting for you to discover it. The more in you wants to be used and not expire with you. It would be a pity if you reached the end of your life only to discover that you have used only three percent of your greatness. The American philosopher Henry David Thoreau captures this best: 'Oh, God, to reach a point of death only to realise that you have never lived'. Can you imagine reaching at the end of your life only to discover that you are dying without using your greatness, without tapping into the more in you, without discovering 'something within you'! Make a resolute decision to live full so that you may die empty. Allow life to use you so that you are able to share your gifts with the world. As St Teresa of Calcutta would say, become a pencil in the hand of God and write a new chapter with your life every day.

Your gift of greatness has the potential to let you live your greatest life. You can get all that you want in any area of your life if you tap into this gift of greatness. People who do not know the value of their greatness are easy prey. I am reminded of President Jomo Kenyatta in his book 'Facing Mount Kenya' where he writes, 'When the missionaries arrived, the Africans had the land and the missionaries had the Bible. They taught us how to pray with eyes closed. When we opened them, they had the land and we had the Bible'. These people in Africa had a treasure in their hands but they did not know it. They did not use it. However, the missionaries knew it, and used it. This is the situation that some of us are in. Greatness is a fortune that we all possess but are unaware of it. We should never let it be stolen from us by our limited vision of who we are. Let nobody, let no circumstance or anything steal your greatness from you.

Face your fears

Most people are not living their greatness because they do not see beyond the horizons of their problems. Anger, frustration, fear, guilt, unhappiness, and resentment often slows down our pace to greatness. These emotions are daily killers and can steal our life from us, making us mentally and physically ill. They require us to be brave and act in spite of our fears.

I am sure that you are not prepared to dwell on your fears forever. I used to but this changed when I met Les Brown. I remember listening to him telling a story of a man who was afraid of a dog in his neighbourhood. Whenever he would pass, the dog would bark and he would run away. One day he decided to face his fear and developed the courage to face the dog. The dog came towards him and he did not run. When the dog reached him, he grabbed it by the collar only to realise it had no teeth. Wow! All those times this man had been running from this dog - it had no teeth! I encourage you to take courage and face your fears. Like the dog, your fears might not have any teeth. Grab your fears by the collar and show them you are unstoppable. Show them you have miracle power within you. Do not let your fears obscure the road to your best self.

I am reminded of my numerous journeys to Rome every year over the past 5 years. Each time I go, I climb over 500 steps to the top of St Peter's Basilica. What has surprised me over the years is that each time I climb to the top, I meet people on the way conquering their fear of heights. Once they reach the top they are happy to see the beautiful horizon.

Dr Patrick Businge

The truth is that not everyone climbs to the top of St Peter's Basilica and sees a new horizon. The truth is that not everyone who climbs to the top of St Peter's Basilica in Rome, the Eiffel Tower in Paris or the London Eye in London challenge themselves to see far. The reality is that we live in a world where most people are prisoners of their comfort zones. I invite you to be different. Have no fear and go beyond your horizon. You will see beautiful vistas that will inspire you to find and manifest your best self. Go ahead and achieve far beyond your horizons. Walk in the avenues of life that you have never explored. In his book 'Secret of the Ages', Robert Collier writes, 'The power to be what you want to be, to get what you desire, to accomplish whatever you are striving for, abides within you. It rests with you only to bring it forth and put it to work'.

It is a fact that many people who would have wished to read this booklet and discover their best selves are already gone before you. Given that you are still alive and breathing, you are still waiting for something special. You are tailor-made for greatness. Make your life count by living every day with purpose. You can do everything with the greatness within you. Join us at Greatness University and we will help you become unstoppable in the pursuit of your greatest life. Thank you for embarking on this uncommon road to find your best self. You are one in a million.

Dr Patrick Businge

BECOME A MASTERPIECE

In this short and powerful booklet you have had a chance to discover three aspects of your best self. I believe that discovering your best self has opened more doors for you to design your greatest life. With this self-knowledge, your life is going to take on a new meaning. Your eyes have opened up to see a new horizon. You have become aware that you are a miracle in manifestation. You have become aware that you are uncommon, unique, and unrepeatable. You have become aware that you are a gift with many gifts.

Now that you are more aware of who you are, you have the power to live your dreams. Do not let your dreams die with you. Remember what Les Brown says: 'The graveyard is the richest place on earth, because it is here that you will find all the hopes and dreams that were never fulfilled, the books that were never written, the songs that were never sung, the inventions that were never shared, the cures that were never discovered, all because someone was too afraid to take that first step, keep with the problem, or determined to carry out their dream'. Develop the courage live life on your terms. Start living full so that you die empty. Have a deep hunger to become a masterpiece because you are a piece of the master. Here are some of the resources that might help you make your life a masterpiece and leave a legacy.

GREATNESS UNIVERSITY

Greatness University was born out of the realization that we live in world where we are sold almost anything and everything except one important product: greatness. So, we decided to become the world's first institution dedicated to discovering, unlocking, and monetising greatness.

We believe greatness leaves clues. We are therefore committed to helping people like you tap into their greatness faster and easier than you ever imagined. We do this by researching greatness in individuals, organizations, businesses, and other spheres of life. We help people like you create their own personal economies by monetising their greatness. We guide people like you on the best ways to create a lasting legacy. Remember, your legacy is not what you give to the people you love but what you live in them.

At Greatness University, we partner with like-minded people to unlock greatness around the world. We offer online courses, run face to face training, give one to one mentoring, and organize boot camps in our areas of expertise worldwide. Our courses and mentoring in the Principles of Greatness, Setting STAR Goals, Live Your Dreams, Walk in Greatness, The Millionaire in You, Speak and Change the World, and Discover the Book in You are not only focused on developing your mind but also speaking to your heart: where your treasure is.

As world leaders, our faculty members are always learning. They are mentored by top experts and great people in the world like Brian Tracy, Les Brown, Omar Periu, and Ona Brown. You have something special. There is greatness within you. Allow us to help you tap into your greatness faster than you ever imagined so that you may make your life a masterpiece. To discover more about our work, visit us at www.greatness-university.com. We look forward to working with you and walking the path to greatness together.

7 STEPS TO GREATNESS SEMINARS

Most people are not living their dreams because they are living their fears. In this foundational training based on Dr Patrick Businge's book titled '7 Steps to Greatness: The Masterplan to Take Your Life, Studies, Career and Business to the Next Level', you will deepen your awareness of the 7 steps that will take the fear out of the process and turn your dreams into reality. You will learn the core strategies Dr Patrick Businge has learnt from his mentors like the world's number one motivational speaker Les Brown and has used in his own personal path from fear to greatness.

When you complete this course, you will:

- Discover the greatness within you
- Develop your mindset for greatness
- Create a formula on finding your purpose
- Design a three dimensional lifestyle
- Develop and use STAR goals
- Deliver your success like all great people.

You have something special. There is greatness within you. Everything you need to live a great life is within you. This training will give you strategies to access your greatness, inspire confidence in your mind, and ignite your heart to go after your dreams.

PUBLISH THE BOOK IN YOU RETREATS

A lot of people want or have at least thought about writing a book. This is because there are a lot of benefits to having a book with your name on it. Writing a book and becoming a published author allows you to position yourself as an expert in your field, increase your credibility, share your message with the world and transform your business. However, few people ever write and publish their book. When you come to our retreat, you will discover that writing your book is not that complicated. We will give you a 7 step roadmap to write, publish and monitise your book. In this roadmap, you will get the strategies that we have acquired from our mentors: Brian Tracy, bestselling author of over 83 books, on how to:

- Discover the book within you.
- Learn the blueprint to write and design your book
- Develop the skills to become a great author
- Publish and promote your book with Greatness University Publishers
- Turn your book into a profitable business

You have something special. There is a book within you. Come to our retreats and discover, write, publish and monetise the book within you. Allow the world to read and be transformed by your message.

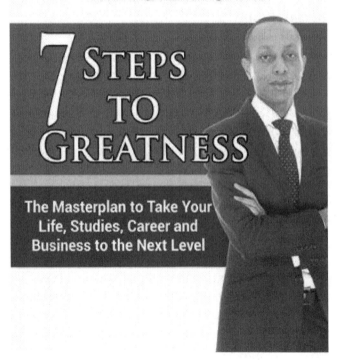

PATRICK
BUSINGE

'This fast moving book is full of great ideas that will
inspire and motivate you to achieve all your goals'.
- Brian Tracy, Bestselling Author.

7 STEPS
TO
GREATNESS

The Masterplan to Take Your
Life, Studies, Career and
Business to the Next Level

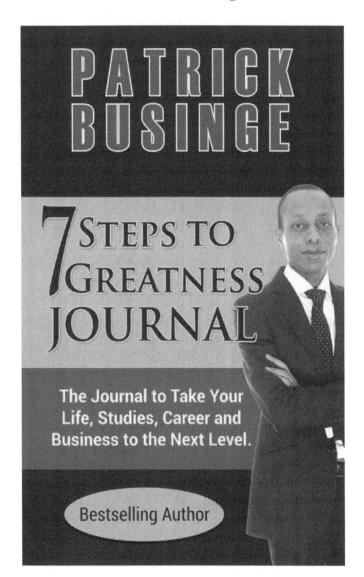

ABOUT THE AUTHOR

Born in Uganda, Dr Patrick Businge did not let his circumstances characterised by war and poverty become his standard. He took steps to raise above his circumstances and made greatness his benchmark.

Dr Patrick Businge is the Founder of Greatness University: the world's first institution dedicated to discovering, unlocking, and monetising greatness in individuals and businesses around the world. His goal is to help you tap into your greatness faster and easier than you ever imagined.

Dr Patrick Businge is an educator. He has taught over 50 000 people in classrooms, churches, orphanages, villages, community centres, and boardrooms throughout the United Kingdom, Europe, Africa, and Americas.

Dr Patrick Businge is an eternal student. He has studied in over 7 universities and acquired over 10 postgraduate qualifications. He has researched, written and spoken for approximately 20 years in the fields of ethics, philosophy, religion, education, armed conflict, disability, and greatness. His ultimate vision is to inspire one million people become instruments of peace, messengers of hope and channels of greatness in this world.

Dr Patrick Businge speaks to corporate and public audiences on the subjects of Personal and Professional

Dr Patrick Businge

Development. His exciting talks, seminars and boot camps on 7 Steps to Greatness, Book Writing, Lead Yourself, Self-Esteem, STAR Goals, Success Mindset and Greatness Awaits bring about immediate changes and long-term results.

Dr Patrick Businge has travelled and worked in over 10 countries on 3 continents. He speaks four languages: English, French, Swahili and some Arabic. Patrick is happily married and has 2 children. He is active in community and national affairs. He has written other books including the sought after '7 Steps to Greatness: The Masterplan to Take Your Life, Studies, Career and Business to the Next Level'. To learn more about his seminars and services, please visit www.greatness-university.com. If you have any personal questions email him directly at info@greatness-university.com or meet him on Facebook, Twitter, LinkedIn and Instagram.

Dr Patrick Businge

Manufactured by Amazon.ca
Bolton, ON